Pieter
BRUEGEL

TELL ME ABOUT

Pieter
BRUEGEL

by John Malam

Carolrhoda Books, Inc. / Minneapolis

This edition first published in the United States in 1999 by
Carolrhoda Books, Inc.

Copyright © 1998 by Evans Brothers Limited
First published in England in 1998 by Evans Brothers Limited, London

Carolrhoda Books, Inc., c/o The Lerner Publishing Group
241 First Avenue North, Minneapolis, Minnesota 55401 U.S.A.

Website address: www. lernerbooks.com

Library of Congress Cataloging-in-Publication Data

Malam, John.
  Pieter Bruegel / John Malam.
     p.   cm. — (Tell me about)
  Originally published: London : Evans Brothers, 1998.
  Includes index.
  Summary: Briefly examines the life and work of the
sixteenth-century Flemish painter, describing and giving
examples of his art.
  ISBN 1-57505-366-7 (alk. paper)
  1. Bruegel, Pieter, ca. 1525-1569—Juvenile literature.
  2. Painters—Flanders—Biography—Juvenile literature.
[1. Bruegel, Pieter, ca. 1525-1569. 2. Artists. 3. Painting,
Flemish. 4. Art appreciation.]   I. Title. II. Series: Tell me
about (Minneapolis, Minn.)
ND673.B73M265   1999
759.9493–dc21
  [B]   98–8486

Printed by Graficas Reunidas SA, Spain
Bound in the United States of America
1 2 3 4 5 6 – OS – 04 03 02 01 00 99

Pieter Bruegel the Elder was an artist. He lived 450 years ago, but no one can be certain when he was born or even what he looked like. He painted pictures of ordinary people working in the fields or playing games or dancing. No other artist had painted such things before, and Bruegel became famous during his lifetime. This is his story.

This drawing of Bruegel was made three years after he died. No one knows if it shows how he really looked. The artist drew it from memory and from some of Bruegel's paintings that might have been self-portraits.

Pieter Bruegel was born in an area of Europe that became part of Holland.

He might have been born in the town of Breda, near the North Sea coast, but we cannot be sure. The year of his birth is also a mystery. It could have been anytime between 1525 and 1530.

Breda, as it looked in Bruegel's time

Nothing is known about Bruegel's childhood. No one has found out who his parents were or whether he had any brothers or sisters.

Perhaps one day an old document, such as a letter, will be found that will help to solve some of these mysteries.

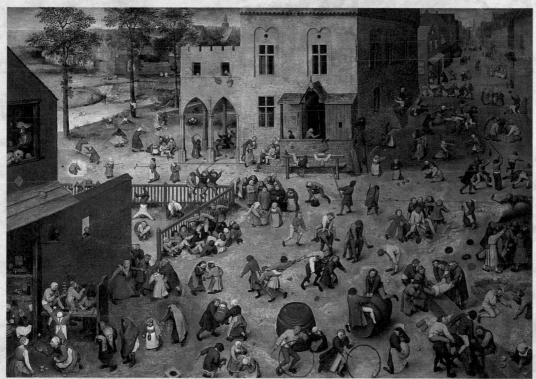

This painting by Bruegel is called *Children's Games*. It shows about eighty different games played by children, such as leapfrog, walking on stilts, and rolling hoops. Bruegel probably played games like these when he was a child.

We do know that at some point, perhaps when he was in his twenties, Bruegel went to live in Antwerp, a big city in present-day Belgium.

In Antwerp he studied with Pieter Coecke. Coecke was a well-known artist who owned a busy workshop. Many apprentices, or students, worked there. It was where they trained to become artists. Bruegel became one of Pieter Coecke's apprentices.

An artist's workshop in Bruegel's time

This British television program showed how artists in Bruegel's time worked. The woman in the center is making blue oil paint.

In Bruegel's time most paintings were made on flat pieces of wood called panels.

Bruegel probably learned how to cover a panel with coats of chalk mixed with glue. When the surface of the panel was completely smooth and white all over, it was ready to be painted on. Bruegel painted using oil paints.

By 1551, Bruegel had finished his training. In that year, he became a member of the Antwerp Guild of Painters. This was like a club, and only fully trained artists could join.

Soon after joining the guild, Bruegel went on a long journey through France to Italy. He was away from home for about two years.

Antwerp as it looked in Bruegel's time

In Italy, Bruegel probably visited artists' workshops and studied paintings. He may have wanted to find new ways to make his own pictures.

But he seems to have been most interested in the scenery he saw on his travels. On his way back to Antwerp, he crossed over the Alps, a range of high mountains. He liked the scenery and he began to make pictures of mountain landscapes.

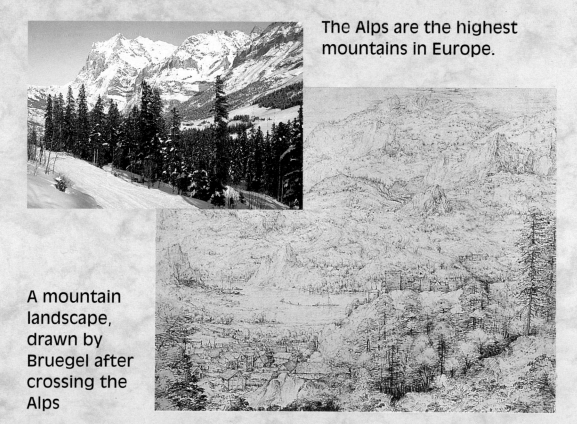

The Alps are the highest mountains in Europe.

A mountain landscape, drawn by Bruegel after crossing the Alps

Back in Antwerp, Bruegel worked for a man named Hieronymus Cock. He was a print maker. Bruegel made drawings, and Hieronymus Cock printed them on to paper. He could make many prints of the same drawing. They were sold to the public.

This print is called *The Big Fish Eat the Little Fish.* In the picture, Bruegel compares people with fish. It is about how big fish (greedy people) swallow up little fish (people who are not greedy).

In 1563, Bruegel married Mayken Coecke. She was the daughter of Pieter Coecke, Bruegel's teacher. They left Antwerp and went to live in Brussels.

Bruegel and Mayken had two sons. They named the older one Pieter, after his father. The younger boy was called Jan. Both sons became artists. Pieter made pictures of goblins and fires. Because of this his nickname is "Hell Bruegel." Jan painted brightly colored pictures of flowers and landscapes. His nickname is "Velvet Bruegel."

Bruegel's son Jan

A flower painting by Jan

Bruegel painted his most famous pictures during the last few years of his life. In a painting called *Mad Meg* (*Dulle Griet* in Flemish), he painted an old woman walking through a strange land full of monsters and bad people. The old woman is carrying bags full of valuable things.

Mad Meg. This painting may have been based on a Flemish saying about a woman who was so greedy and bad that she could steal from hell without fear.

Paintings based on Bible stories were popular with artists in Bruegel's time. In his painting *The Tower of Babel,* Bruegel showed the tower described in

Genesis, the first book of the Bible.

Bruegel made the tower look like a famous Roman building called the Colosseum. He had seen it when he visited Italy.

(Above) The Colosseum, in Rome

The Tower of Babel. Which parts look like the Colosseum?

Bruegel's paintings are full of detail. In *The Hunters in the Snow,* a group of hunters are returning to their village in winter. One hunter is carrying the fox they have caught. In the distance people are skating on frozen ponds. Some are playing ice hockey, while others are spinning tops. Still others are building a fire.

The Hunters in the Snow probably shows the month of January. Other paintings by Bruegel represent different months.

Another painting that shows a winter scene is *The Census at Bethlehem* (or *Numbering at Bethlehem*). In this picture, Bruegel made Bethlehem look like a village in Holland, and not like the Bethlehem of the Bible.

Mary and Joseph are at the bottom of the picture. They are arriving by donkey at an inn. A crowd of people wait to be counted as part of the census.

The Census at Bethlehem. Look for the little hut with the cross on its roof. Bruegel might have meant this to be the stable where Jesus was born.

Bruegel earned the nickname "Peasant Bruegel," because he liked to paint pictures of the ordinary people he saw in Holland. In *The Wedding Dance* he painted about 125 people dancing and talking in a forest clearing after a wedding.

The Wedding Dance. Look for the bride. She is in the middle of the picture, wearing a garland in her long red hair. She is dancing with an older man, who may be her father.

In another wedding picture, called *The Wedding Banquet* (or *The Peasant Wedding Feast*), guests are enjoying a feast.

The bride sits with her back to the cloth on the wall. But which man is her new husband? Perhaps it is the man passing the dishes from the serving board. Or perhaps it is the man leaning back from the table, calling out for more drink to fill his empty jug.

The Wedding Banquet. The serving board is actually a door. You can see its metal hinge.

Pieter Bruegel the Elder died in 1569, at about forty. A writer named Carel van Mander wrote about him in a book in 1604. He said:

"Bruegel was a very quiet and thoughtful man, not fond of talking, but ready with jokes when in the company of others. He liked to frighten people, even his own pupils, with all kinds of spooks and uncanny noises."

This drawing by Bruegel might be a self-portrait. He might have had long hair and a beard, and he probably did wear clothes like these.

Important Dates

The letter *c* before a date means "about."

c.1525–30	Pieter Bruegel the Elder was born in what became Holland
c.1545–50	Learned about painting from Pieter Coecke
1551	Became a member of the Guild of Painters in Antwerp, a city in present-day Belgium
1552–53	Traveled in Italy
1554	Visited Switzerland, where he made drawings of the Alps
1555–63	Lived in Antwerp, painting and drawing
1560	Painted *Children's Games*
1562	Painted *Mad Meg*
1563	Married Mayken, the daughter of Pieter Coecke, his teacher. They moved to Brussels
1563	Painted *The Tower of Babel*
1564	Son Pieter was born
1565	Painted *The Hunters in the Snow*
1566	Painted *The Census at Bethlehem*
1566	Painted *The Wedding Dance*
1567-68	Painted *The Wedding Banquet*
1568	His son Jan was born
1569	Pieter Bruegel the Elder died, in Brussels

Key Words

apprentice
someone who works for, and is taught by, a teacher

landscape
a painting or drawing of the countryside

oil paint
a type of paint made by mixing a color with oil from a plant

panel
a flat piece of wood on which a painting was made

print
a copy of a picture on paper

self-portrait
a picture that an artist makes of himself or herself

Index

Acknowledgments

The author and publisher gratefully acknowledge the following for permission to reproduce copyrighted material:

Cover Musée des Beaux Arts, Caen, France/Bridgeman Art Library
Back cover Mary Evans Picture Library
Title page Kunsthistorisches Museum, Vienna/Bridgeman Art Library
page 5 Mary Evans Picture Library **page 6** Alan Jacobs Art Gallery, London/Bridgeman Art Library **page 7** Kunsthistorisches Museum, Vienna/Bridgeman Art Library **page 8** Private Collection/Bridgeman Art Library **page 9** © BBC **page 10** Christie's, London/Bridgeman Art Library **page 11** (left) Robert Harding Picture Library (right) The Pierpont Morgan Library, New York **page 12** Graphische Sammlung Albertina, Vienna **page 13** (left) AKG (right) AKG London/ Erich Lessing **page 14** Museum Mayer van der Berg, Antwerp/Bridgeman Art Library **page 15** (top left) Adam Woolfitt/Robert Harding Picture Library (bottom right) Visual Arts Library **page 16** Kunsthistorisches Museum, Vienna/ Bridgeman Art Library **page 17** Musée des Beaux Arts, Caen, France/Bridgeman Art Library **page 18** Visual Arts Library **page 19** AKG/Erich Lessing **page 20** Visual Arts Library

About the Author

John Malam has a degree in ancient history and archeology from the University of Birmingham in England. He is the author of many children's books on topics that include history, natural history, natural science, and biography. Before becoming a writer and editor, he directed archeological excavations. Malam lives in Manchester, England, with his wife, Hilary, and their children, Joseph and Eve.